ARMIES OF THE PAST

GOING TO WAR IN THE
18th CENTURY

GOING TO WAR IN THE
18th CENTURY

PAUL COOPER

W
FRANKLIN WATTS
A Division of Scholastic Inc.
NEW YORK TORONTO LONDON AUCKLAND SYDNEY
MEXICO CITY NEW DELHI HONG KONG
DANBURY, CONNECTICUT

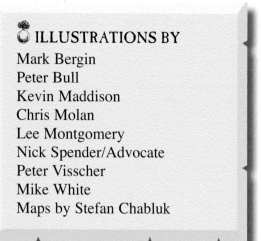

ILLUSTRATIONS BY
Mark Bergin
Peter Bull
Kevin Maddison
Chris Molan
Lee Montgomery
Nick Spender/Advocate
Peter Visscher
Mike White
Maps by Stefan Chabluk

Editor Penny Clarke
Editor-in-Chief John C. Miles
Designer Steve Prosser
Art Director Jonathan Hair
Picture Research Susan Mennell

First published in 2001 by
Franklin Watts
96 Leonard Street
London
EC2A 4XD

First American edition 2001 by Franklin Watts
A Division of Scholastic Inc.
90 Sherman Turnpike
Danbury, CT 06816

Catalog details are available from the Library of
Congress Cataloging-in-Publication Data

ISBN 0-531-14593-X (lib. bdg.)

Printed in Hong Kong/China

CONTENTS

18TH-CENTURY WARS

For much of the 18th century, Europe was at war as countries fought each other to increase their territories. As a result of the War of the Austrian Succession (1740–48) and the Seven Years' War (1756–63), Prussia (modern Poland and northeast Germany) and Russia became major European land powers. France tried to become a major world power but was defeated on land by the Prussians and at sea by the British. Britain won territory in Canada and India, mainly from the French.

RUSSIAN TERRITORY

BRITISH TERRITORY

Seven Years' War 1756–63

American Revolution 1775–82

SPANISH TERRITORY

13 AMERICAN COLONIES

MAJOR WARS AND LEADERS 1740–92

Frederick the Great of Prussia

King George II of Britain

King George III of Britain

George Washington first U.S. president

The War of the Austrian Succession 1740–48
Under Frederick the Great, Prussia invades the Austrian province of Silesia. Many world powers become involved in the war.

The Seven Years' War 1756–63
Frederick the Great declares war on Austria and Russia. Britain, ruled by King George II, defeats French forces in North America.

War around the globe 1739–63
France and Britain fight each other for control of colonies (overseas territories). The British defeat the French at sea and overrun their colonies.

The American Revolution 1775–82
Britain's American colonies rise in protest at paying increased taxes, sparking the American Revolution. This leads to the birth of the United States.

WORLD MAP c.1770

NORTH SEA

BRITAIN

POLAND

War of the Austrian Succession 1740–48

PRUSSIA

Seven Years' War 1756–63

SILESIA

War of the Bavarian Succession 1778–9

BOHEMIA

FRANCE

BAVARIA

EUROPE c. 1770

AUSTRIA

BRITAIN

POLAND

PRUSSIA

War in Eastern Europe 1787–92

RUSSIA

ATLANTIC OCEAN

FRANCE

AUSTRIA

SPAIN

OTTOMAN EMPIRE

AREAS OF BRITISH CONTROL IN INDIA

INDIAN OCEAN

Emperor Joseph II of Austria

Catherine the Great

Louis XVI of France

The War of the Bavarian Succession 1778–79

When Austria meddles in Bavaria's affairs, Prussia invades the Austrian territory of Bohemia (now part of the Czech Republic). The two armies are evenly matched, and the war is brief.

War in Eastern Europe 1787–92

Russia, ruled by Empress Catherine the Great, wins several victories against the Ottoman (Turkish) empire and gains large areas of land from Poland. Russia becomes a powerful nation.

The French Revolution, 1792

France is racked by revolution. The French king, Louis XVI, has been executed and replaced by a republican government. The major world powers prepare for war against the French government.

RECRUITING

In the 18th century, army recruits were often teenagers. Sometimes army recruiters traveled around fairs and market towns, hoping to pick up men looking for work.

Today it is hard to understand why so many young men chose to sign up for such a tough job, but life at home could be desperate for poor young men. There were few other jobs available. Sometimes the choice was to join the army or starve. If you were male, fit, and tall enough, the army offered food, shelter, clothing, and some pay — as well as the chance of adventure.

MARKET DAY

The soldiers of the local recruiting party wore their dress (best) uniforms while a band of military musicians played stirring tunes. The recruiters told potential soldiers how wonderful life was in the army and how it was their duty to join up and serve.

In wartime, men could be "impressed" — forced to join the army. Impressing men was a good way for local authorities to get rid of young troublemakers and hooligans.

A British army recruiting party signs up young men in a town on market day.

British ensign

RANKS FOR SALE

In the British army, the officers who commanded ordinary soldiers had to pay for their rank, so only wealthy men could hold top positions.

At the time of the American Revolution, the lowest rank of officer, ensign, cost £400 — a huge amount of money.

PRUSSIA

Every Prussian man could be called for military service, but many exemptions were granted. After an initial six months' training, each recruit had to spend two months per year drilling with his regiment — except during wartime, when continuous service was required.

The king's shilling

GIVE AND TAKE

New British recruits got a payment of about seven pounds. They were also given a shilling coin called "the king's shilling" to signify that they were now in the pay of the king. They had to spend most of this money on equipment, however.

REGIMENTS

Armies of the 18th century were organized into regiments. In many countries, the names of regiments reflected the area of the country or state in which the men were recruited. In Germany, for example, the Hesse-Hanau Infantry Regiment fought for the British in the American Revolution.

LOCAL MILITIA

In North America, there were no permanent armies like those in Europe. Instead there were local defense forces called militia. Men were called up for a year at a time to fight if necessary. If there was no fighting, they just had to turn up occasionally for drill practice.

AMERICAN MILITIAMAN

Short coatee

Smoothbore flintlock musket

Breeches

INFANTRY

BRITISH INFANTRYMAN c. 1775

Infantrymen are the ordinary foot soldiers of any army. In battle, their job is to take and hold ground, following all orders by their officers. In an 18th-century battle, they fired volleys of lead shot before advancing toward the enemy.

Each regiment organized its infantry into companies of between 30 and 70 men. Each company had officers to give orders and non-commissioned officers (NCOs) to make sure the orders were carried out.

UNIFORMS

The picture on the right shows a "private" — short for "private gentleman," the lowest rank in any army. Privates in all 18th-century armies carried similar equipment.

MUSKETS

Every 18th-century infantryman had a flintlock musket that fired round lead balls. Each ball, together with its charge of gunpowder, was contained in a paper cartridge. Muskets had a maximum range of 330 feet (100 meters), but were only accurate to about 100 feet (30 meters).

OTHER WEAPONS

Most ordinary soldiers carried a bayonet, a stabbing weapon that fitted over the end of the musket. After firing a musket volley, troops might be ordered to make a bayonet charge — run at the enemy soldiers and stab them to death. Some soldiers also carried short swords known as hangers.

Image labels:
- Woolen coatee
- Facing color on coatee, different from unit to unit
- Belt
- Waistcoat
- Breeches
- Muzzle-loading musket
- Bayonet
- Linen gaiters to protect legs
- Leather shoes

FIRING A MUSKET

Ramrod

Priming pan

LOAD!
Infantrymen were drilled to load and fire their muskets as quickly as possible. Each soldier rammed the gunpowder charge and lead ball down the barrel with a metal ramrod.

PRIME!
Then the soldier filled the musket's priming pan with gunpowder. He closed the pan and cocked the weapon so that it was ready to fire. Then the soldier took aim.

FIRE!
When he pulled the trigger, the flint held in the jaws of the spring-loaded cock struck sparks and ignited the priming powder in the pan, which set off the main charge and fired the ball.

Prussian grenadier

IN CHARGE
Each company had officers, such as the captain below, to lead it into battle. Officers were granted a commission (authority to perform military duty) by their government. They usually wore more elaborate uniforms than enlisted men.

American captain

German

French

FLANK COMPANIES
Every infantry regiment had special units called flank companies that could tackle tough jobs. The tallest and strongest soldiers joined the grenadiers. Fit, slim men joined the light infantry.

THE COLORS
Regiments had large flags known as colors, which were carried into battle for troops to rally (gather) around when ordered. This was useful because soldiers could easily become confused by the clouds of smoke and the noise of battle. The colors were defended by a group of soldiers called the "color party."

CAVALRY

Most armies contained cavalry regiments. These were soldiers who fought on horseback. There were two types of cavalry — heavy and light.

In battle, heavy cavalry charged at the lines of enemy infantry, making a gap and riding through it to cut down as many troops as they could to force a retreat. Light cavalry was used for small-scale fighting or "skirmishing" and to observe the enemy's troop movements.

HORSES

Cavalry horses had to be large and strong enough to carry a trooper and all his equipment. They were cared for at the regiment's stables. The saddle, harness, and regimental decorations they wore were known as horse furniture.

Heavy (left) and light cavalry troopers attack enemy infantry.

INTO BATTLE

At the start of a battle, the cavalry waited tensely for the order to charge. When it came, they rode at full gallop toward the enemy. It was important for charging cavalry to stay together, but they often broke formation in the excitement of smashing through the enemy's front line.

TACTICS AND TRAINING

The best way for foot soldiers to repel a cavalry attack was to form densely packed squares bristling with bayonets. The enemy's horses would refuse to ride into the sharp bayonet points.

When they were not fighting, cavalry troopers spent their time training. They practiced staying in formation and using their weapons properly. They also trained for ceremonial riding in official parades.

British troops, formed into a square, attempt to repel an American cavalry charge.

WEAPONS

Cavalry troopers carried a large saber (curved sword) designed for slashing down at the enemy from horseback. Such swords often had a cagelike hilt known as a basket hilt, which protected the trooper's hand from enemy saber cuts.

Cavalry troopers also used muskets called carbines. They were shorter than infantry muskets so that they could be fired from horseback. A pair of large-caliber "horse pistols" in saddle holsters completed the cavalryman's formidable array of weaponry.

Cavalry carbine

Horse pistol

Basket hilt on heavy cavalry saber c. 1780

Light cavalry saber c. 1790

Light cavalry saber scabbard

ARTILLERY

In the 18th century, artillery (big guns) supported infantry on the battlefield, battered down the walls of forts, and smashed enemy ships at sea.

There were many different types of artillery. The smallest, field guns, had two-wheeled carriages so their crews could move them around easily. The biggest, massive siege guns, were moved with great difficulty by teams of oxen.

18TH-CENTURY FIELD GUN

- Touch hole
- Cast bronze barrel
- Muzzle
- Steel rim on wheel
- Field carriage
- Cannonballs
- Gunpowder
- Rammer
- Wheel

FIELD GUNS

In a battle, field guns helped the infantry by blasting gaps in the enemy's front line. Big guns were described by the weight of shot they fired. For example, a "six-pounder" fired an orange-sized iron cannonball weighing 6 pounds (3 kg).

LOADING AND FIRING A CANNON

READY!
To load a gun, the crew first pushed the cartridge (a canvas bag) full of gunpowder down the barrel with a rammer. Then they pushed down the shot, followed by a cloth wad to stop the ball from rolling out.

AIM!
The gunner pierced the cartridge through the touch hole, then filled the touch hole with fine priming powder. The crew aimed the gun, and the gunner blew on a burning match held in a holder called a linstock.

FIRE!
When the gunner put the match to the touch hole, the priming powder exploded, setting off the main charge. This sent the cannonball shooting toward the enemy. Then the barrel was sponged out to extinguish any sparks.

SPECIAL ARTILLERY

BOMB KETCH
To bombard a coastal target, navies used a ship called a bomb ketch. A large mortar, mounted in the middle of the ship, lobbed the bombs onto the shore.

HOWITZER
Another type of special artillery was the howitzer. These guns fired exploding shells high in the air so that they crashed down on a target.

MORTARS
Armies laying siege to a fortress or town used a special type of high-angle cannon called a mortar to fire exploding bombs over the walls. "Coehorns" were small, portable mortars.

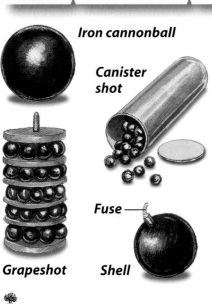

Iron cannonball

Canister shot

Grapeshot

Fuse

Shell

⚜ TYPES OF SHOT
Artillery pieces fired many different kinds of shot. There was solid shot for general use. Shells exploded on impact and destroyed forts or buildings. Grapeshot consisted of about two dozen tennis-ball–sized iron balls that flew apart on firing. Canister shot was a large tube filled with musket balls.

Mustapha fires the cannon.

⚜ WHAT A CLEVER BOY!
According to legend, at the battle of Fontenoy in 1745, a gun crew's mascot dog, named Mustapha, watched as his masters were killed by enemy fire. Leaping onto the gun with the smoking linstock in his mouth, he set off the charge that destroyed a large company of advancing French troops.

SPECIAL DUTIES

Every 18th-century army employed special soldiers. Mercenaries worked for whichever country would pay them. Pioneers cleared land. Surgeons treated the wounded, and musicians conveyed orders in battle and played tunes to keep spirits up on the march.

In the British army, drummers were also responsible for flogging (whipping) soldiers who had misbehaved. Other soldiers guarded prisoners of war, who in the 18th century were often held in terrible conditions.

British pioneer

PIONEERS

Pioneers were builders and diggers who cut down barriers and built defenses. Each pioneer wore an apron and carried an axe.

American drummer

DRUMMER

Drummers and buglers were vital in a battle because they conveyed orders. Their loud rhythms and notes could be heard over the confusion, and different drum beats and bugle calls meant different things. Regimental drummers could be boys as young as 10 or 12 years old.

German mercenary from the Waldeck Regiment

MERCENARIES

Soldiers sometimes joined foreign armies as mercenaries. Some went because their government had made a treaty to send troops to support a nation already at war. Forces from many German states fought alongside the British in America. French troops fought with the Americans.

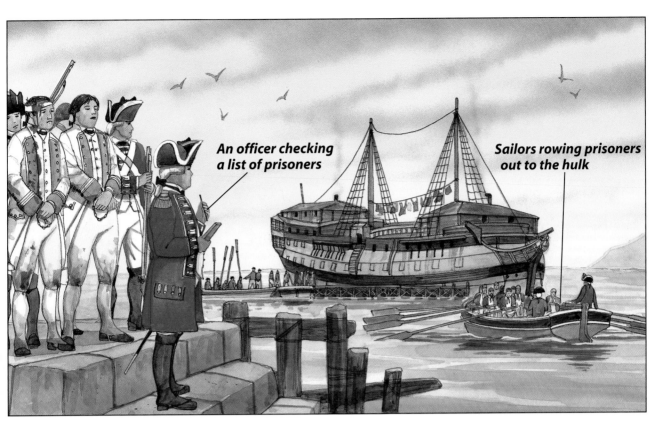

An officer checking a list of prisoners

Sailors rowing prisoners out to the hulk

 ## PRISONERS

Enemy troops held as prisoners in wartime could be treated very badly. During the American Revolution, British forces kept American prisoners in prison hulks (unused ships) anchored off New York City. Americans kept British prisoners down in a copper mine.

Prison hulks were old ships permanently anchored near a shoreline or in a river.

PUNISHMENT

If a soldier disobeyed orders or became drunk while on duty, he could expect harsh punishment. This was usually flogging with a cat-o-nine-tails — a whip made from knotted cords that quickly cut open the skin.

Other punishments included being tied to a wagon wheel for hours or being pilloried (trapped in a wooden frame while people threw things at you). Death by hanging was the punishment for spying or turning traitor.

For even small offenses, a soldier could expect to receive 100 lashes.

THE AMERICAN REVOLUTION

After the British defeated the French in North America in the Seven Years' War, the British government demanded that its 13 American colonies help pay for the war. The colonists, who were already heavily taxed, objected. Fighting began in 1775.

In 1781, the main British army surrendered at Yorktown. The peace treaty that followed led to the colonies' independence and the birth of the United States of America.

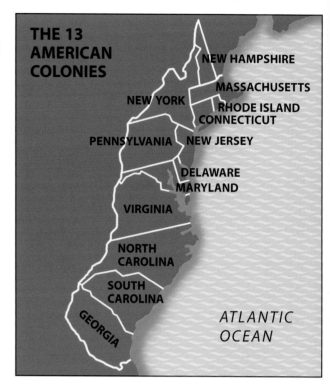

THE 13 AMERICAN COLONIES

NEW HAMPSHIRE
MASSACHUSETTS
NEW YORK
RHODE ISLAND
CONNECTICUT
PENNSYLVANIA
NEW JERSEY
DELAWARE
MARYLAND
VIRGINIA
NORTH CAROLINA
SOUTH CAROLINA
GEORGIA
ATLANTIC OCEAN

Minuteman

COLONIAL MILITIA
Before the Revolution, each colony had its own militia. Often called minutemen because they could be ready to fight at a minute's notice, these volunteers formed the backbone of the colonial forces that first fought British troops.

AMERICAN RIFLEMEN
Many colonists in the frontier areas of America were armed with hunting rifles instead of the smoothbore muskets used by conventional armies. Although slower to load than the musket, the rifle was far more accurate. A good marksman armed with a rifle could pick off soldiers at a range of at least 650 feet (200 meters).

Colonial rifleman

British troops suffered heavy losses at the Battle of Bunker Hill.

BATTLE OF BUNKER HILL

Fought close to the city of Boston, the Battle of Bunker Hill (June 17, 1775) was the first major battle of the Revolution. British troops marched out of Boston to attack American defenses. Two attacks were thrown back, but a third British attack forced the Americans to retreat. British forces suffered heavy losses, proving that the American colonists would not give in easily.

AMERICAN INDIANS

Although both sides employed American Indian warriors, the British used them the most. American Indians were skilled scouts and raiders in wooded frontier regions.

SCALPS AND SCALPING

The practice of scalping — the removal of the skin and hair from the tops of enemies' heads — was widely used by American Indians and other frontier fighters. Reports of Indian tribes fighting for the British and taking scalps were exaggerated by the Americans to create anger toward the British.

A British soldier loses his scalp.

FORTS AND SIEGES

After the Middle Ages, the use of artillery made high-walled castles obsolete. They were replaced by forts with thick, low walls able to resist gunfire.

To make 18th-century forts more difficult to capture, extra defenses, such as bastions (triangular projections), were added to the main wall. Artillery within the fort covered all angles of attack. No fortress was impregnable, however. If the attackers had enough resources and time, even the strongest fort would fall. Some sieges went on for months.

CROSS SECTION OF A FORT'S DEFENSES

Outside the fort

Covered way

Scarp

Parapet

Inside the fort

Ditch

Firing platform

Ditch walls lined with dressed stone

A map of the fortifications surrounding the French town of Nîmes in the 1600s

VAUBAN
Sébastien Le Prestre de Vauban (1633–1707), a French engineer and soldier, was the greatest fortress-builder of his time. The types of fortresses he designed were used throughout the 18th century. Although he adapted each design to the site, certain features were common to most fortresses. A few are shown above.

FORT DESIGN
Fort designs often resulted in structures that were star shaped (left). The sharp angles of the walls allowed defenders to cover all the areas outside the walls with gunfire. Enemy troops attempting to storm the fortress had to cross a killing ground. In the 18th century, such troops were known as the "Forlorn Hope."

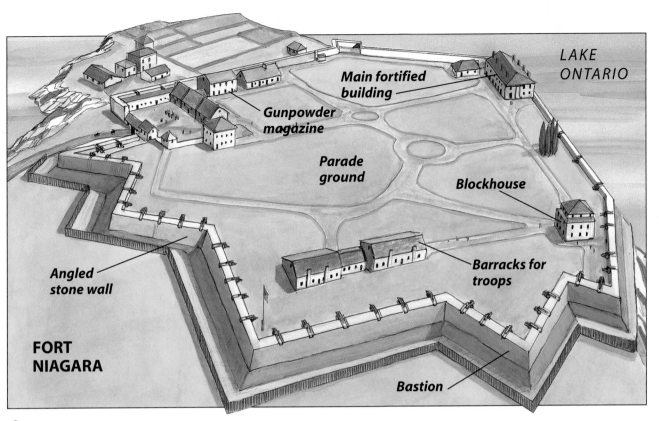

FORT NIAGARA

Main fortified building

Gunpowder magazine

LAKE ONTARIO

Parade ground

Blockhouse

Barracks for troops

Angled stone wall

Bastion

FORT NIAGARA

Many forts built in North America during the 18th century were simple and made from tree trunks. The French fort at Niagara, however, was built along the lines of one of Vauban's forts.

Work on the structure began in 1726 and was completed in the 1750s. Situated on a peninsula between the Niagara River and Lake Ontario in what is now New York State, the fort's main defenses are on the landward side.

SIEGE EQUIPMENT

BARBETTE CARRIAGE

In the 18th century, Jean Baptiste de Gribeauval, a French artilleryman, developed the barbette gun carriage for use in forts. The cannon on the carriage fired over the parapet.

GABIONS

Gabions were wicker cylinders. During sieges, they were filled with earth and piled up to protect the besiegers from being shot by the defenders.

CHEVAL DE FRISE

The cheval de frise was first used during the siege of Groningen in Friesland (now part of the Netherlands) in 1658. It consisted of huge stakes protruding from a wooden base. It stopped cavalry attacks.

TACTICS

Infantrymen were the backbone of 18th-century armies, as battle tactics were based on the movement of foot soldiers. Infantry had to be able to move across the battlefield in orderly lines and fire their guns in a disciplined way.

The side that won an 18th-century battle was almost always the one with the most disciplined infantry. That is why Frederick the Great of Prussia was so successful — he had the best-trained foot soldiers in Europe.

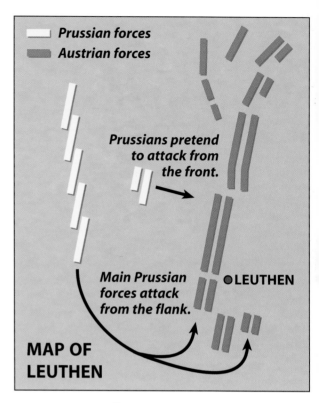

Prussian forces
Austrian forces

Prussians pretend to attack from the front.

●LEUTHEN

Main Prussian forces attack from the flank.

MAP OF LEUTHEN

A TYPICAL 18TH-CENTURY ORDER OF BATTLE

Commanders at rear

Artillery positioned in gaps in between infantry lines

Infantry positioned across the battlefield in firing lines

Cavalry positioned at the flanks

🎖 BATTLE OF LEUTHEN

One of Frederick the Great's favorite battle tactics was to pretend to attack from the front, but then send most of his forces to attack one of the enemy's flanks (sides). At the battle of Leuthen (December 6, 1757), this tactic won the day. By the time the Austrian commander realized that his left flank was being destroyed by the Prussians, it was too late.

🎖 BATTLE ORDER

To prepare for a battle, generals normally drew their troops up in long lines with the infantry in the center. Cavalry was positioned on the left and right flanks of the infantry, with artillery behind the gaps. When battle began, the infantry advanced slowly toward the enemy, while the cavalry attacked the enemy troops.

The members of the first company have just fired their muskets and are reloading.

The second company is firing.

The third company waits to fire.

🔥 SHOOTING BY NUMBERS

Although the infantry of each country had slightly different ways of firing, the British system was fairly typical.

Rather than fire all their muskets at once, the companies of the battalion were organized into three "firings," each of three companies. The first "firing" fired a volley and began to reload; then the second firing occurred, followed by the third firing. By this time the men of the first firing had reloaded and were ready to fire again.

🔥 FIX BAYONETS!

Most battles were won because one side had superior firepower, but some officers believed the best way to defeat the enemy was to charge at them with fixed bayonets.

In the Prussian army, Frederick sometimes forbade his infantry from firing on the enemy at all, insisting they attack only with bayonets. However, this tactic only worked if the Prussian artillery had already inflicted heavy casualties on the enemy.

Prussian grenadiers charge with fixed bayonets.

LIFE IN CAMP

Even in wartime, soldiers were not usually engaged in fighting battles. Most of their time was spent in military camps. These huge tent cities housed thousands of soldiers, who might spend weeks or even months under canvas.

Armies in the 18th century moved slowly, and generals tried hard to make sure their troops were properly supplied with food and equipment. Before a campaign began, commanders set up magazines (supply centers) along the route of the march.

IN CAMP

While they were in camp, soldier had a chance to relax and enjoy themselves. After the soldiers had completed their training and othe tasks of the day, they would sit around the campfire, eating and gambling.

Medical tent

Commander's tent

Officers' tent

Tethered horses

AN ARMY IN CAMP c. 1775

Soldiers on guard duty

FOOD SUPPLY

An army, which might consist of between 50,000 and 100,000 men, needed a vast amount of food. In the Prussian army, huge herds of cattle followed the army on its campaign. In wartime, each soldier was supposed to receive a free loaf of bread every day, but he had to buy meat and other food from his own pay.

⚜ BILLETING

In peacetime, most soldiers lived in the homes of civilians. Although the government was supposed to pay for this, billeting was generally very unpopular. The pay was poor (usually late), and the soldiers often behaved badly. Toward the end of the 18th century, the building of barracks — permanent buildings to house soldiers — began.

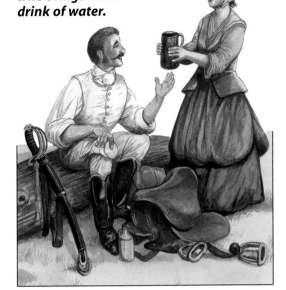

A cavalry trooper's wife brings him a drink of water.

Soldiers' tent

Supply wagon

⚜ ARMY WOMEN

A few women accompanied soldiers on campaign. Some were soldiers' wives, but most women served as cooks, laundresses, and nurses, or acted as sutlers — tradespeople who sold food, drink, and other provisions to soldiers in the camp.

An officer dances with a young woman at a ball.

⚜ OFFICERS AND ENTERTAINMENT

Most civilians feared the presence of large armies because soldiers regularly stole food and belongings. Officers, however, were generally welcomed in the homes of well-off people. They were most popular among young women, many of whom thought officers were very handsome and might even make good husbands. Regimental bands often provided music for local dances.

LIFE IN THE NAVY

French naval captain

For an 18th-century nation, control of the sea and the riches of the East meant enormous power. For most of the century, Britain, France, and Spain were engaged in fighting each other at sea.

Sailing even a small man-of-war required large numbers of men, so navies always needed volunteers. Life for a sailor could be even harsher than that of a soldier.

🌀 TOP OF THE TREE

A naval captain (right) had to take strong command. A captain who was too lenient risked losing the respect of his crew members, but one who was too harsh was in danger of a mutiny (uprising). Sailors, like soldiers, were punished with flogging.

SPECIAL CREW MEMBERS

MARINES

Sailors were not the only crewmen on board — there were also soldiers called marines. In a battle, they fired their muskets or helped to board an enemy ship.

"POWDER MONKEYS"

In battle, boys as young as seven ran between the cannons on deck and the magazine in the bottom of the ship, bringing fresh cartridges to the gun crews.

SURGEONS

A skilled ship's surgeon was indispensable. He operated below decks on men wounded in battle, amputating arms and legs shattered by cannon shot and flying splinters.

BATTLE TACTICS

Ships attempted to pound each other into surrender by using broadsides (firing all the cannons on one side of a ship). If a damaged ship refused to surrender, a party of marines and sailors would attempt to board the vessel and fight it out on deck.

French and British warships fire broadsides at each other (above).
New sailors are kidnapped by the press gang (below).

BIG AND SMALL

In the 18th century, ships were classified according to how many guns they carried. A "first-rate line-of-battle ship" had as many as 120 cannons. Frigates, with around 32 guns, were much faster. Navies used them as escorts to larger ships.

THE PRESS GANG

Britain's Royal Navy was so short of men that "press gangs" were sent out in wartime to kidnap able-bodied men for naval service. As experienced seamen were highly prized, merchant (civilian) sailors might be impressed on their way home after months at sea.

AFTER THE BATTLE

The major European states, such as Prussia, Austria, and France, maintained large armies. At the end of a war, the soldiers in these armies returned to their towns and worked as farm labor — but they were always ready to fight again.

The British disbanded most of their forces at the end of a war. After the Seven Years' War, the British army was reduced from nearly 200,000 men to 45,000 almost overnight. This kind of drastic cut often caused great hardship, as ordinary soldiers suddenly found themselves out of work and poor.

A disabled ex-soldier begs in the street.

Byng is executed on the deck of his own ship.

A GRIM FUTURE?

Many old or disabled soldiers who had been forced to leave the army lived in desperate poverty. Governments sometimes set up hospitals and workhouses to look after them. In Britain, the Chelsea Hospital in London — founded by King Charles II — cared for 440 old soldiers.

SHOT!

Most defeated commanders were not punished. One exception was the British admiral John Byng. In 1756, he was sent to the Mediterranean to fight the French, but after an indecisive battle he withdrew. Because of his failure to defeat the enemy, Byng was found guilty of neglect of duty and shot by a firing squad (left).

VILLAGE TALES

The British East India Company used native soldiers, called sepoys, in their army to help them govern parts of India. When old sepoys left the army, they returned to their villages. They were encouraged to tell their stories to persuade young men to join up.

A sepoy tells villagers stories about life in the army (right).

PRACTICAL HELP

General John Manners, Marquis of Granby, was a British commander in the Seven Years' War. After the war, Granby spent a lot of money setting up old soldiers as landlords of inns. Many pubs in Britain today are still called the Marquis of Granby.

BACK TO THE FARM

In Prussia, soldiers returned to their towns and villages when the fighting was over. There they went back to working at their trades or as farm laborers, tilling the land and harvesting crops until the next period of drilling with their regiment began.

FAME AND FORTUNE

For successful commanders, war could bring great rewards. The soldier who achieved the greatest success at the end of an 18th-century war was George Washington. He led his forces to victory in the American Revolution and became the first president of the United States.

George Washington, painted in 1782

29

GLOSSARY

Artillery
The large guns of an army and the soldiers who maintain and fire them.

Bayonet
A sharp stabbing weapon that fitted over the end of a musket.

British East India Company
The organization that effectively ran large parts of India on behalf of the British government during the 18th century. It had its own army.

German mercenary

Cannons
Nonportable firearms with long barrels and a caliber of more than 20 mm.

Carbine
A short, light gun, originally designed to be used by cavalry.

Cavalry
The mounted soldiers of an army.

Color party
Hand-picked soldiers who defended the regimental colors from capture by enemy forces.

Colors
Elaborate flags carried into battle by a regiment. They provided a rallying point for troops disoriented by smoke and noise.

Commission
The document that gave an officer authority to perform military duty.

Ensign
The most junior rank of officer, whose duty was to carry the regimental colors.

Flank company
A group of specially designated soldiers within an infantry regiment who fought together and supported the other companies.

Flogging
Whipping, as in punishment for breaking army or navy rules.

Frigate
A type of light, fast 18th-century warship.

Grapeshot
Cannon ammunition that consisted of a cluster of small iron balls separated by wooden discs. The balls scattered after firing.

Grenadier
The tallest and strongest soldiers in a regiment, who fought together as a flank company.

Howitzer
A type of cannon that fired an explosive shell at a high angle so that it crashed down on the enemy.

Infantry
The foot soldiers of an army.

Light infantry
The fittest and cleverest soldiers in an 18th-century army, who fought together as a flank company.

Man-of-war
A general term for an 18th-century wooden warship.

Militiamen
Civilians who volunteered for military training to provide a home defense force and to swell army numbers in wartime.

Minuteman
A nickname for an American soldier from the time of the American Revolution, so called because he could be ready to fight at a minute's notice.

Mortar
A short cannon that fires an explosive bomb at a very high angle.

Musket
A long-barreled, muzzle-loading shoulder gun in use from c. 1650 to the mid-1800s.

Muzzle-loader
A gun in which the ammunition is pushed down the barrel through the muzzle.

Officer
A soldier above the rank of regimental sergeant major.

Press gang
A gang of soldiers or sailors whose duty was to seize civilians and force them to join the army or navy.

Private
The lowest rank in any army.

Ramrod
A wooden or iron rod used to push ammunition into the barrel of a gun.

Regiment
A large, permanent military unit, usually comprising a number of battalions and often further divided into companies.

American drummer

Saber
A long, curved, single-edged sword designed for use on horseback.

Sepoy
A native Indian soldier in the army of the East India Company.

Shell
Hollow artillery ammunition filled with either explosives or pieces of metal.

Sutler
A tradesperson who sold food, drink, and other items to troops in camp.

INDEX

PICTURE CREDITS
Peter Newark's American Pictures p. 29

**Indianapolis
Marion County
Public Library**

Renew by Phone
269-5222

Renew on the Web
www.imcpl.org

For general Library information
please call 269-1700.